i wonder...

a collection of poems

Alice Smith

Here is what people are saying about Alice Smith's poetry.

"Alice Smith's poems are like the roof crashing in or the ground swelling up. You're surrounded by ordinary things - a marriage, a mother and her dog, a sanitized front lawn, - when suddenly, things explode. In one line or a handful of words, Smith is able to transform the everyday into the sacred and the beautiful. That is the gift of poetry, and Smith reminds us to pay sweet attention to the small things before us. That's where the meaning is."

David Cook - columnist for the Chattanooga Times Free Press

Alice Smith lures us across the threshold of her secret inner world, a world which we quickly recognize as our own. Whether walking in the woods or down a wedding aisle her poetic offerings bring our own secrets to consciousness where they can be embraced and honored. Good poems serve this essential mysterious purpose, and these soul-full selections meet the test.

Jerry R. Wright - Jungian Analyst

Alice Smith's voice is one to be heard. Her words evoke feelings of wisdom and truth, of delight and regret, as she writes about coming full circle in life. She writes of coming of age, and compares her two marriages, showing disappointment without a trace of bitterness. She marvels over the good in life. Her words bring the reader to despair, then describe hope and the beautiful shining moments of life so clearly it is palpable.

Ferris Kelly Robinson, author of *Dogs and Love - Stories of Fidelity*, and *Never Trust a Hungry Cook*

These poems are about this very moment, and yet they also (and sometimes at the same time) go way back, way forward, and way deep--with beautiful, fresh metaphor and surprise at all the right places. Once you start you are pulled through to the end. What a pleasure to read and learn about yourself—taught by the poems, the art, of a poet who is exploring everything within reach, and learning about herself.

   Clyde Edgerton, author of Walking Across Egypt *and* The Night Train

Alice Smith's collection of spare, beautiful poems actually functions as a memoir, the faithful record of a conscious life. Family forms the constant yet ever-changing circle of her world, as love brings joy, then pain, then joy again. A woman's journey is mapped in these pages, and an enviable wisdom is born. As all good poetry does, Alice Smith's poems have made me look at my own life in a more attentive and appreciative way.

   Lee Smith, author
   Hillsborough, NC

A Clear Night

The moon so bright
I can see
my shadow
underneath.
No city lights
to distort the darkness
and diminish
the sparkling
spectacle above.
Seemingly solid
streaks and splashes
of stars are painted
across the sky.
Lost in wonder
with no desire
to find the exit,
I humbly marvel
at the enormity
of what this night
is showing me
and what more is
out of sight.

Big Fat Question Marks

I don't know
what I don't know,
but I know it is
enormous.
Trying to punctuate
the unknown
with periods
feels like wearing
control top
pantyhose.
I'd rather let it
all hang out
and give
my big fat
question marks
plenty of room
to breathe.

A Scar

Welcome pleasures
fly through frequently
but leave no scars
when they fade
from memory,
but pain produces
a noticeable gash
and hangs around for a spell.
Just when the wound
begins to scab,
something rips it
open again
allowing the blood
to seep from the skin
and stain the white
cotton robe.
Another bandage
is applied,
and healing resumes.
Curing continues
until all that remains
is a scar.

The Sign

JESUS
a single word
painted on a piece
of wood
and nailed
onto a tree.
Every time I see
the sign
I want to stop
and paint one
of my own.
I never do.
I just look
and wonder
what might
hang under.
Leroy?
Sammy?
Rhonda?
Tammy?
Maybe one day
I'll simply paint
a question mark
and hammer it below.

Mid-winter

Woolen wraps
and cashmere caps
protect us from
the frigid outer air.
Bitter cold
that numbs the nose
and creates
involuntary tears
makes mid-winter
a bleak and dreaded
time of year.
But ah, the bare beauty
of winter trees!
Every limb exposed
and every twisted twig
an individual
piece of art.
The cruel cold
strips away
the loaded leafy layer
hiding the complex
branches underneath.

Spring is Coming

Today I saw yellow in the woods.
Premature promises
pushing through
the brown leafy carpet
fill me with hope.
Each new bud and sprout
I see makes me know
winter is about to take a bow.
I'm flushed with floral fever
though the cold is hanging on.
Knowing more winters
lie behind me than ahead,
I'll rip off my wrap
and embrace the present
beauty about to blossom.

Gloom and Bloom

April showers
bring May flowers,
an all too familiar saying
describes a way of paying
attention to raining sorrow
that brings a joyful tomorrow.
Patiently listening to thundering sadness
can clear the clouds covering gladness.
There is no way to push away the gloom
to hurry the long awaited bloom.
The darkness and the light
are both a part of the plight.

Doubt

Concrete certainty
solidifies
fluid possibility
and stultifies
natural evolution
diminishing
the mystery and wonder
of the Divine.
Doubt creates
the rising question
that leavens the bread,
the fruitful searching
that ferments the wine,
and the endless exploring
that finds the unexpected spark
of light in the darkened tomb.

Giving Up Giving Up

Once I was asked to produce a piece
for the church's lenten pamphlet
and was sent a wretched and joyless
Old Testament passage
as a source of inspiration.

My contribution was titled
"I Hate Lent",
and the good news is
no one has asked for
another submission from me.

I'm giving up the giving up.
To hell with silent penitence!
Instead of delving into deprivation
I'll sing from the spring
welling up inside of me.

Holding Hands

Both are wearing Sunday shoes.

One dressed in polished wingtips
  is sitting still in church.

The other wearing well worn sneakers
  is wandering through the woods.

His spirits rise
  when soprano descants
  soar above the melody.

Her soul is nurtured
  by nature's unwritten undertones.

Two divinely driven beings
  walking in different shoes,
  plowing separate paths
  are both holding hands
  with the holy.

Inside Out

Curious unknown people
want a part of me,
but interaction with strangers
drains me dry and leaves me limp
like a torn and tattered rag doll.
The world prefers the extrovert
who gathers strength and energy
from the outer,
relishing the chance of running
into someone or something new.
I live from the inside out,
hunkered down at home,
puzzling with the mystery inside me,
playing with the pieces I see,
putting them together in poetry.

Imagine

Night was drawing nigh
when it caught my eye:
a peace sign drawn
on the dirty window
of a bumper-sticker minibus.
From the numerous displays
I imagined the owner to be
a wispy haired granola girl
hanging out at GNC.
I couldn't get enough
of what she had to show.

Plant seeds. Sing songs.
Knot your hair not your mind.
Excuse me while I kiss the sky.
Hate sucks.
Don't harsh my mellow.
I'm boldly going nowhere.
Normal - just a dial on the washing machine.
Nature is my church.
All who wander are not lost.
Be more like Muir.
I can't tell if I'm enlightened or just don't give
a shit.
Who would Jesus bomb?
Love is all we need.

He was walking towards me in the dark.
The man was big and black and burly.
His hooded head was bowed
so I couldn't see his face.
I'm more a fan of Muir than malls,
but I was grateful for the
multitude of mall rats
scampering to their SUVs
in case this suspect human being
was coming after me.
He climbed inside the minibus.
I shook my head and smiled
at what I had imagined.
I'd like to know the bumper sticker guy,
but I guess I never will.
As he backed out of the parking space
I threw him a finger sign of peace.
He rolled down his dusty window
and flashed one back at me.

Middle Ground

I want to be
wowed by wonder
knocked to my knees,
tickled to tears,
and possessed by passion
all the time,
but I'm not.
I don't want to be
devastated by disaster,
crushed by criticism,
trampled by tragedy,
or lost in loneliness
all the time,
and I'm not.
I have
glimpsed the glorious
and tasted the terrible,
but most of the time
I muddle around
in the middle.

My Daughters

In law
Grand
Step
In law
Grands
Leapt
into my life.
I love every one of them,
but I gave birth to none of them.
Thanks to the men in my life
for giving me my daughters.

Denial

Lying in bed
only half awake,
a single word
clearly came to me.
        DENIAL
I could actually see it
written in the air,
but instead of grabbing it
I pushed it off
on someone else I knew
who used it regularly
to wrap what was unwanted
and tie it up with a capital D.

Months later
when I was lying
in the same bed,
he stood there
and ripped the present open
so I couldn't help but hold
        that word.
I thought it belonged to another,
but it clearly belonged to me.

Left Overs

The dream
has become
old and stale,
but it keeps appearing
on my plate.
The dream giver
serves it
over and over
hoping I'll discover
a hidden taste
of freshness
in this heap of
left over mess
I long to throw away.

Once Upon a Time

Once upon a time
has many different endings.
Happily ever after
is rarely true to life.
When the princess weds the prince
there is majesty in the moment.
This is where the story stops,
tho there is so much more to come.
The middle has a million scripts
where happiness has its place,
but it's balanced by a darker space
that contains the pain and sorrow.
All we really know of once upon a time
is they lived to face tomorrow.

Two Little Words

It was a simple response
with an empowering effect.
I was in my own little world
soaking,
relaxing,
unwinding.
A door slammed shut,
and a voice called up to me.
"Did you remember to get some milk?"
Shit!
I had forgotten.
I always bought the milk,
but he was the only one who drank it.
I tensed,
feeling failure
bubbling up from below.
Then I answered
"No..... DID YOU?"
The simple addition of two little words
let me go on
soaking,
relaxing,
unwinding.

Part of the Brilliance

I rose with the sun
and slept beneath the stars.
The strength of my son
and the rushing river
carried me along by day,
but at night
I lay on the beach
at the bottom
of the Grand Canyon
feeling alone and apart,
dumped and disconnected,
separated
from the comfortable familiarity
that no longer described my life.
Then I caught sight of shooting stars
sailing through the summer dark,
and my sense of
separateness
dissolved.
No matter what,
I was part
of the brilliance
that creates and sustains
the evolving universe.
I hiked with my son
out of the Canyon
and into the rest of life.

Loving Leaving

I love my husband's former wife
for leaving him.
When she moved out
he moved on
and found his way
to me!

Living On

The first time around
they couldn't see each other
for it was bad luck.
She was upstairs dressing.
He was downstairs waiting.
The organ hidden in the family den
was played by a rented stranger.
Joyful music had been requested,
but a funereal sound filled the air
as her father walked her down
and handed her away.
The boy in black and the girl in white
recited solemn vows
and thumb wrestled in secret
while they were holding hands.
No one can remember now
which thumb won,
but twenty eight years later
the marriage lost.

The second time around they dressed together
in the house that would become their home.
Her dress was the color of his pale blue eyes.
His suit a version of the grayer blue of hers.
This time her father was seated with her mother
as the couple walked together down the aisle
to the joyful sound of a friend's guitar.
The man & woman looked into each others eyes
and repeated sacred vows without the word obey.

At ceremony's end Isaiah's blessing was read:
"You will go out in joy and be led forth in peace;
the mountains and hills will burst forth in song
before you,
and all the trees of the field will clap their hands."
Spontaneously friends and family broke into
applause,
while arm in arm the couple left to strumming
alleluias,
and the marriage is living on.

The Sum of What We Are

8-1
4+3
2+2+2+1
However you calculate it
there are seven.
We celebrate
the sum of what we are,
and the joy of being together
has multiplied over the years.
We cannot escape
the fact that our days
are numbered.
There's sadness in subtraction,
but the time will come
when we are only 6
then 5
then 4
then 3
then 2.
I hope I'm not around
when we've dwindled down to
1.

My Fix-it Man

I left the old, dark place
and moved into a house
where light pored in every window
and the smell of new permeated the air.
The beautiful home was lacking something,
but space was not the issue.
I found someone who pointed out
the house was missing a shop.
What woman wants a shop?
All the tools I need
live in a catch-all drawer.
If I can't hammer it or screw it
a phone call solves the problem,
but this time calling a fix-it man
wouldn't do the trick.
My repair required 24 hour service.
The one I wanted to do the job
was the one who wanted a shop
so I agreed to create a space for him.
Now it overflows with
a mess of manly merchandise
waiting to be used.
He had what it took to fill that space,
and whenever something comes apart
I praise his power tools
then hug my very own fix-it man
for knowing how to put things back together.

One of the Stars

In a scene from Immortal Beloved
I watched Beethoven
become a star.
He was wearing
a white nightshirt
when he crawled from
his bedroom window
and ran through the darkness
to the backyard pond.
He leapt into the liquid
and floated in the starry
sky reflected in the body
of water.
There was no script
or dialogue,
only the sound of
Ode to Joy
as the camera
ascended higher
and higher,
and the man
became a star.

Shut Up Wisdom

Knowledge speaks,
but wisdom listens.
Even ignorance tries
to voice itself as truth,
and if spoken
with a certain tone
can often fool the listener.
Tedious talking
incessantly pounding a point
can feel like a jackhammer
trying to crack through the skull.
As you pass through life
you will have many opportunities
to keep your mouth shut.
Take advantage of all of them.

Bleeding Through

Dream life bleeds into waking life,
  and the other way around as well.
Someone threw it out,
  a cracked plastic Solo cup
  disturbing the nature
  of the woods.
Red on the outside.
White on the inside.
Out of place
  in its leafy brown surroundings.
My first reaction,
  disgust over thoughtless littering.
My second threw me
  into the dark of a dream
  littered with images,
  red and white.
Blood spilling from Mama's head.
Crimson staining milky white.
Red pooling underneath the pillow.
Unlike the empty cup,
  thoughtlessly discarded,
  the dream was full
  and thoughtfully thrown out
  for careful handling.

Going to the Movies

It tortures me to watch torture
on the screen.
When knowing conscious cruelty
is part of the picture
I choose to stay away.

It pains him to see
irrationality in play.
When he is blindsided
by illogical beings
he cringes, shifting in his seat
knowing he cannot beat
some logical sense
into a head that thinks
a different way.

I can delve into damage
of the psychological kind
feeling curiosity about
this sort of mind.
He can see a character
callously carving or blatantly beating
another human being
without having to get up and leave.

Each of us knows
what the other wants
to avoid
so we seek out
mutually satisfying ways of
sitting in the dark together
escaping for a while.

Please Exclude Me

Uh-oh!
Why did he mention
The Stuffed Owl,
an anthology of bad poetry?
I glanced through several
hysterical collections of bad
then fearfully cringed
at the thought of being included.
Most of what I write
I see as mediocrity
compared to the truly great,
but maybe I'm fooling myself
and using an inflated description.
What if I'm really bad?
But wait.
It looks like you have to be
famous and critically acclaimed

for a lifetime of work
that is undeniably good
before you can be
slashed and burned
for producing a verse or phrase
that is pretentiously, laughably bad.
I think I'm safe.

The Bus Bitch

I knew it was a miserable idea
the moment it was mentioned.
The excursion advertised itself
as being a luxury tour. The problem?
Being closed up in a traveling, temperature
controlled contraption forced to listen
to a guide clutching a microphone telling
me what is passing me by is my idea
of a journey conceived by a sadist.
I've tagged myself a bus bitch,
much preferring to breathe in
foreign and familiar fragrances
and hear the sounds of nature,
or saunter down a side street
while I feel the outside air blowing
through my hair. Even in a car
I can stop and look and listen whenever I
wish,
but the bus driver will only let me out
to capture a touristy photo op.
All said, I agreed to give the tour a try.
I climbed aboard and settled into my
luxury seat and felt claustrophobia
closing in. My traveling companions,
well aware of my aversion, looked at me
and could easily see what I was feeling.

When the piercing voice of the guide
penetrated my space with her spiel, I bolted.
Hell, who wants to see Cartagena?
One who experienced the tour in full
ended up envying me - The Bus Bitch
who had the balls to bolt.

The Dealer

Sitting in front of a computer
compulsively playing bridge
imprisons the viewer in mindlessness.
When empowering the machine
to deal what is seen,
the player is lost in a lazy losing game.
If the creative card comes into play
the viewer reclaims a bit of control.
Fingers trip from key to key
playing a different kind of bridge
that leads to a place where the cards
are constantly shuffled and rearranged
by the dealer deep within.

Wearing the Weather

The weather wears on me.
My calendar claims
it's spring,
but I see
a dreary winter sky
peeking through
the blinds
making me feel
cold and grey.
Instead of dressing
in olive drab,
today I'll try to
trick myself
and wear the weather
I choose.
I'll put on red and purple,
dotted with chartreuse,
let bright break through
the overcast
and look like
a Redbud
just about to bloom.

Unnatural and Nearly Unbearable

Sweltering southern summers
can make it hard to breathe
so we hopped a plane to Maine,
but Mother Nature threw us a curve.
It was ninety five degrees!
Unnatural and nearly unbearable.
We wanted what came before
this wilting withering weather.
Where was refreshing cooler air
like spring in Tennessee?
Traveling northward we finally found
restoring, blessed relief.
Camden was idyllic, beautifully blending
what man had built and nature had provided.
We hovered around the harbor
and soaked in our surroundings.
Then something took my breath away,
and I couldn't help but stare.
Unnatural and nearly unbearable!
Too little meat covering her bones,
too much tan coloring her skin,
too few wrinkles enhancing her face,
two enormous mounds of flesh
constructed on her emaciated chest.
If she'd embraced what nature had provided
I might have never stared.
Perhaps that was the problem.

We All are One

To hell with cooking!
Let's go out.
We three women and our two men
love to share a meal
especially when none of us
has to be preparing.
Our single friend
always tells the server,
"I'm one person."
One night I couldn't help myself
and said,
"I'm one person too".
Being part of a couple
doesn't make me
any more or less of a person
than someone living alone.
Last time she smiled at me
before announcing,
"I'm one check."
The server heard her "I'm" as "on"
and put it all together.
It matters not who pays for what
because we all are one.

Enough

Truly sad are those
who have so much
yet see their bounty
as never quite enough.
Lucky are the ones
who have so very little
and see themselves
as being blessed with plenty.

Dying Words

After my father died
my mother read six words
over and over and over again.
You're in my thoughts and prayers
may be fraught with feeling,
but to her this phrase had lost its life
and reeked of rigor mortis.
She wanted to dig a hole
and bury these worn out words
six feet under.
Reliving her reaction
has made me dig for different
words to tell a grieving person
You're on my mind and in my heart.

Disturbing the Peace

A screaming ambulance
came crashing through
my meditation
disturbing the peace
and trying my patient side.
I took a breath
and slowly let it go
knowing the driver
of the disturbance
was unaware of me
and trying his best
to save the patient inside.

Creativity, Simplicity and Balance

CREATIVITY
sparks imagination
bringing something new to life,
expanding beyond the bounds
of what is here in sight.
SIMPLICITY
calls for paring down
and letting go
of cluttering complications.
Excessive creativity
can lead to sheer exhaustion
where overdone simplicity
can end in nothingness.
The tension between
expansion and contraction
brings to life a necessary
BALANCE.
The elder women of Saint Anna
take these sacred vows
practicing and projecting
the beauty of Godly aging.

Simply Being There

When my father died
the Lhasa howled,
the children cried,
but Mom put off her grieving.
After the funeral
we sucked our mother into smoking,
not something we often do.
We hoped to help her blow away the pain,
but the mourning party was too much for her
so she took her little dog to bed and cuddled
what she had shared with Dad.

Years later she was sitting on her porch
wearing sunny morning yellow,
holding that little Lhasa on her lap.
Tears were messing up my face
as I watched my mother carry
her little love and climb into my car.
I never knew how long a drive half a mile
could be.
The vet was kind.
The death was peaceful,
but not for Mom and me.
We sobbed and hugged,
not something we often do.
We took the same route home, but it was
even longer.

She said she'd lost her link to Dad.
I nodded, but I wondered,
What was I?
Over and over she thanked me
for simply being there.

That morning death was the overture
to a motherless symphony.
Off and on all day I cried and tried
to drown out the deadly drum.
She was home alone, sitting in sunset yellow
when I walked onto her porch
and she sucked me into smoking.
Together we inhaled the morning sadness,
and I tried to blow away the pain.
One day I won't be able to thank her
for simply being there.

Waiting

Waiting
for the verdict
or the diagnosis
or a birth
or a phone call
or a crying baby to fall asleep
or a lost dog to wander home
or worries to wander away
or a marriage to be dissolved
or a loved one to appear
or a trip to begin
or a life to end.
Waiting is part of living.
Sometimes waiting enhances what's to come,
and sometimes waiting simply sucks!

Wedding Picture

The Family Farm nestled in the redwoods
was a fairytale setting for a summer wedding.
I was pretty in pink sitting beside my spouse.
A little farther down the pew
sat my former husband with his wife in blue.

I watched my son as he waited for his bride
to join him under the trees
and recite creative vows.
He swore to feed her sweets forever.
She pledged to be his playmate.
When the married couple kissed,
the clapping couldn't wait.

We gathered in the woods for pictures.
First the family of the bride,
Then the family of the groom
which was later divided in two.
We were forming groups
 as we were told to do.

The groom requested a picture
with his father and his mother.
The camera recreated
something from the past.
Our son was in between
blending together the three.
When we parted he said,
"Thanks for making me."

Don't Fly Away

standing on the dock
with buds in my ears
listening to Hummingbird
surrounded by music and memories
so different from the tiny creature
in the song
darting and whizzing
through the air
my father's
large familiar
khaki form
calmly paddling toward
the fallen trunk
whip-sound of the rod
line floating through the air
fly landing precisely
in a hidey hole
between branch and bank
where he knows the treasure lives
swimming beneath the surface
the voice
plugged in my ears singing
don't fly away, don't fly away
over and over again
fading out into silence
as he slowly vanishes
with the song.

At Last

She changed her repertoire
and smoothly shifted
into songs from Nat
and Natalie Cole.
Then she borrowed
one from Etta James
and sang for us
At Last.
Her new found tone and rhythm
were sung in my father's key
who loved to settle back
with Ella and Sinatra.
If only he could be here
and feel her velvet voice,
but his stroke erased that verse
so we had to modulate.
She came to him
with her improvisation,
transposing a sickly home
into a lively, harmonious lounge.
He missed a beat every now and then
lip syncing all the way.
Now when I remember him
wrapped up in her magic
I cling to what she gave us.
Joyful peace at last.

Clearing the Clutter

She howled in the home
that was no longer her own.
The childhood place
was rid
of physical reminders
of belonging.
The hollow
devoid of decoration
swallowed her
and spit her into
a wailing wake
saturated with sadness
and something more.
Clearing the clutter
left plenty of room
for moving on
into a future
full of freedom
mingled with
monumental memories.

Be Yourself

Dare to be yourself.
It's the only you there is.
Do not weep and wail
when your imitation
of another fails.
Look in the mirror
and risk reflection.
Dig as deep
as you can go.
Who knows
what gold or garbage
lingers below.
Experience fully
all that crosses your path.
Develop your dreams
to see your scars.
Live your life
as only you can do.

Playing a Part

On stage
my character
has been created
by someone
I have never met,
and this someone
guides me
to inner territory
often unexplored.
Scripted words
easier to project
than those of
my own making.
The undesirable
and extraordinary
easier to display
veiled as fiction.
Praise to the power
of playwrights
for uniting me
with foreigners from within.

Being in Doubt

I was a nun for a while
looking inside
to find that certain part of me
afraid to dabble in doubt.
Being the one
who knows what's right
takes a toll on one and all.
I tried to hold on
to my habit,
but when all was said and done
I had doubts.
I had such doubts.
Thank God I never took
Catholic vows
or lived in a nunnery.
I only wore a costume
and prayed in front
of an audience.
When the final act was over
I left the stage of certainty
knowing I needed doubt.

Who Knows?

Tomorrow might be
a day just like today,
warm and sunny and bright,
encouraging sprouting jonquils
to show a yellow hint of spring.
Who knows?

We might get another snow
covering all in sight
in a blanket of white
but breaking branches
with beautiful unbearable weight.
Who knows?

Meteorologists make a living
telling us what's to come.
Sometimes they're spot on
and sometimes they are
flat out wrong.
Who knows?

Maybe the world
will come to an end
the way the forecasters
of rapture predict
every now and then.
Who knows?

It's possible that those of us
who don't see eye to eye
will one day share a big umbrella
and walk around together
underneath a rainy sky.
Who knows?

What Do You Do?

My glass was half empty
when I saw them headed our way.
Everyone at the cocktail party
was famous for something.
Well almost everyone.
What would I say to
"What do you do?"
I was a stay at home mom,
a term not yet invented.
Maybe I could stretch the truth
and call myself an actor
or flat out lie and say
I used to be an astronaut.
When the noble novelist strutted over
with the serious documentarian
I knew my time was up.
They looked at my sister first
to ask the dreaded question.
She glanced at one and then the other
then shook her hair and said,
"I'm the mother of four,
have full time help,
play tennis every day
and recently had my color chart explained."
The question never came my way.
I smiled and sipped
from my glass half full of Chardonnay.

Crashing into the Threat

A window separated us.
When they flew by
he caught my eye
before I noticed
there were two.
I tore my eyes from him
and took a look at her,
delicately balanced
and blended into the background,
wearing what she'd been given,
unable to perk up her appearance
even if she'd wanted.
Somehow I felt pity for her plainness.
Though they bore the same name
and sang the same song
the two appeared to be so different.
The flashy red one couldn't help
recapturing my attention.
He cocked his head and noticed a threat
coming from my direction
then flew at me and crashed
into his own reflection.

Saving Thyme

A long time ago
the grass included so much thyme
the children's dirty clothes
were herb scented
after rolling down the hills
for hours at a time.
Someone got the notion
to purify the lawn.
No wandering weeds or fragrant herbs
would mingle with the grass.
It wasn't going to be the way it used to be.
But that thyme had meaning to me!
When I squished a couple of sprigs
between my fingers
I could smell the children's clothes
or taste the corn and tomato salad
the herb would later flavor.
During the herbal eradication
I found a living patch of thyme
mixed into the moss meandering
onto a small stone bridge
and begged that it be left alone.
There's not as much as
there used to be,
but every summer I go to the bridge
to check on the thyme I saved.

Headed Home

I feel left out, like I don't fit in
so I decide to head for home.
I walk to the river bank
thinking I can swim across,
and that will get me there.
The water is deeper
and the current stronger
than I anticipated.
I am swept off my feet
before I can turn around.
I'm terrified I'm going to drown.
It's useless to try to swim upstream
so I let my body go limp
fearing all the while I'll be attacked
by something underneath.
I make a conscious effort to
stay still
while floating on my back.
I'm fast approaching the other side
but fear being dashed into
the large sheer cliff ahead.
I am much relieved to arrive downstream
where I drag myself up
the embankment to safety.
I see a dirt path and start
walking down it
not knowing where it will take me.

Blessing of Silence

For the mystery that enfolds us
and blesses us,
For the beauty that surrounds us
and nourishes us,
For the life that flows within us
and among us,
For the bounty before us,
We bow.

If pressed to say a blessing
I rely on the one above,
but given a choice
I usually decline
for I know the Divine
is present in the silence.
Sharing a meal in and of itself
is a holy prayer.
Listening to life
blesses whatever is there.

Looking for Some Light

I think I can.
I think I can.
Right now
I think I can't.
Who am I to say
I can't?
I'm not the one
who's badly broken
or in need of surgical repair.
And the world is filled
with billions
far worse off than I.
My immediate woes
are but a faint whisper
to those who wonder
when or if
their children will be fed
or their brothers will be dead
so should I raise my head,
sing a song,
dance along,
wear ribbons in my hair,
make believe that life is fair?
I can't pretend
to ignore my plight,
but maybe tomorrow
I can see some light.
I hope I can.
I hope I can.

I Wonder

I FOUND IT
A bumper sticker
  displayed with pride
  for all the world to see.
I never got it
  for what I need is mystery.
I can't find all the answers,
  but I keep on
  asking questions
  that push me deeper
  into places
  that fill me up
  with wonder.

The Magnifying Glass of Loss

For everything
that's taken
something new is given.
Look through
the magnifying glass of loss
to see the larger picture.
Watch youthful exuberance
shrink gracefully
into an ever expanding perspective,
and see how nimble knees
that used to run with ease
can take a bow to
mental flexibilities.
Examine flowering physical energy
wilting into the space
the withering has created
for fertile reflection.
Observe almighty stardom
as it plays to multiple standing ovations
then learns to curtsy with humility
as the curtain slowly closes.

Alice Smith lives in Chattanooga, Tennessee with her husband Alfred and their dog Leroy. She is the author of **A Place Where Secret Shadows Shine**.

CPSIA information can be obtained
at www.ICGtesting.com
Printed in the USA
BVHW041144010720
582737BV00013B/191

9 781499 692471